LION

BY TYLER GRADY

Dylanna Press

Lions are **mammals** that can be found in sub-Saharan Africa. Although they were once spread across the continent and even found in Europe and Asia, the majority now live in Eastern and Southern Africa.

They are related to cheetahs, jaguars, tigers, and other types of cats. Their scientific name is *Panthera leo*, which means roaring lion.

---

mammals – warm-blooded animals with hair or fur that give birth to live young

One of the most recognizable members of the animal kingdom, lions are known for their loud roars, which can be heard up to five miles (8 km) away!

Lions are one of the biggest members of the Felidae family, second only to the tiger in size. They weigh between 300 to 550 pounds (136 to 250 kilograms) and average 5 to 8 feet (1.5 to 2.5 meters) in length with an additional 2 to 3 foot (.6 to .9 meter) tail. Males are much larger than females.

Lions have long muscular bodies with shorter legs, a large head, and small rounded ears. Their yellow-gold fur is thick and short and they have hairy tufts at the end of their tails. Male lions have distinctive shaggy manes.

The lion's primary **habitat** is a grassland, **savanna**, or woodland area. An area that provides natural cover is ideal as it provides a hiding place for lions when hunting their prey.

Lions live in hot climates where temperatures usually range between 68 to 86°F range (20 to 30°C). Summers are wet and winters are dry.

---

habitat – surroundings or conditions in which an animal lives

savanna – grassy plain with few trees with tropical or subtropical temperatures

The lion has many physical adaptations to its environment.

The color of their fur helps them to blend in with their surroundings and acts as camouflage. This makes it easier for them to sneak up on their prey.

They have very sharp eyesight and a strong sense of smell, both of which allow them to find and stalk their prey.

Lions also have sharp claws and teeth which allow them to tear and chew meat. All of these qualities make them excellent hunters.

___

adaptations – ways in which a species becomes fitted into its natural environment to increase its chance of survival

Lions are **carnivores**. They mainly hunt and eat medium to large herbivores such as zebras, antelopes, and wildebeests. However, they have been known to kill animals ranging from rodents to elephants.

In addition, lions will **scavenge** any meat they can find including taking fresh kills from other animals such as hyneas.

Male lions eat an average of 15 pounds of meat per day, females consume on average 10 pounds per day. A lion is capable of eating 15 percent of its bodyweight during one meal.

_____

carnivore – animal that only eats meat

scavenge – to take from unwanted or discarded material

Female lions do the majority of the hunting. They often work together in groups to catch their targets but can also hunt alone.

They will **stalk** their prey or wait in camouflage for one to walk by. When the prey animal is within striking distance they charge and kill by a bite to the neck or throat.

They are able to run very fast but only for short bursts, so they rely on the element of surprise. They will give chase but only for a short distance.

Lions typically hunt at night or dusk and their night vision is excellent. They hunt every 2 to 3 days but can go for up to a week without eating.

---

stalk – follow an animal's movements

Lions are **polygamous**, with both males and females mating with more than one partner. Mating takes place year round and usually not until the lion is 4-5 years old.

The gestation period is around 110 days. Lion babies are called cubs. A mother lion will typically give birth to three cubs (can range from 1 to 6). Baby lions are very small, blind, and helpless when born.

Lionesses will keep their cubs hidden for about six weeks. She will then introduce them to other members of the pride. Other lionesses may help look after the cubs.

The mother lion looks after her cubs and teaches them to hunt. By the time they are two years old they are independent.

---

polygamous – having more than one mate at a time

Male lions do not have a big role in the raising of their offspring. It is the mother lioness who feeds, protects, and teaches her cubs to hunt.

The male lion's role is to protect the pride, including the cubs, from threats such as predators, and guard their territory against outside intruders.

This is important because if a male lion loses his dominant status in the pride, the new dominant male will kill all of the existing cubs in the group.

When male cubs are grown, they are typically chased off by the dominant male of the pride.

Lions love to sleep! They are the laziest of the big cats, spending as much as 16 to 20 hours per day sleeping and relaxing.

Lions are generally **nocturnal**, conserving their energy during the day when it's hot and becoming more active during the cooler nights.

They do not live in dens or caves, instead they will sleep in open areas or seek refuge from the sun under trees. Lions can also climb and will relax in the low branches of trees.

Only mother lions about to give birth will seek out a den area for her newborn cubs.

---

nocturnal – active at night, asleep during the day

Lions are very social animals and are the only big cats to live together in groups, called prides.

A pride is composed of five or six related female lions, their cubs, and one or two male lions. The pride works together to defend its **territory** and protect the young.

Members of a pride communicate with one another through a variety of **vocalizations** such as roars, growls, and purrs.

They also use body language such as rubbing their heads together to bond and spread their scent.

---

territory – area of land that belongs to an animal

vocalization – the sounds an animal makes

The average lifespan of a lion in the wild is 10-15 years, with females living longer than males. They can live twenty years or more in captivity.

The total population of lions left in the world is approximately twenty thousand. This is much lower than the estimated 200,000 of a century ago.

The lion population has been on the decline for many years and they are considered a **vulnerable species**.

---

vulnerable species – species considered to be facing a high risk of extinction in the wild

Lions are at the top of the food chain. A fully grown lion faces no predators in their natural habitat, making them **apex predators**. However, young or sick lions can become victims to hyenas, leopards, and jackals.

Humans are the biggest threats to lions. Expanding human populations threaten lions through habitat destruction. Poaching by humans for the illegal wildlife trade also contributes to lion deaths.

Another risk facing lions is **climate change**. Extreme weather conditions and drought make food harder to find.

---

apex predator – an animal at the top of the food chain

climate change – long-term changes in weather patterns

Lions are beautiful and majestic animals. They are symbols of courage and strength and have earned their nickname as king of the jungle.

Unfortunately, lions continued existence is under threat due to loss of habitat, hunting, and climate change.

Conservation efforts are underway but it remains to be seen if this amazing big cat can survive in the coming decades.

---

conservation – protecting natural resources for future generations

Word Search

```
N O I T A T P A D A K E M B B
W C M A S B U C H J G A A R W
I F S F F X E E I A N N N H K
M E Q T P R D T L B N N E U J
P N S W P I I F H B J A P N K
W V R P R O U C E X E V R T S
I I P P E O L Q A R Z A E E L
L R I U M C F Y O U A S D R A
A O N A I E I V G Q L G A W M
N N C M A Y I E X A F X T D M
R M H C B N O E S D M Y O E A
U E M G R B L G D S F O R I M
T N O A K H X U G Q G V U R Q
C T C S C A V E N G E E L S C
O U Y I U N A P S E F I L L Y
N H Q L G C X W S W A L C P E
C O N S E R V A T I O N E F R
D H A B I T A T X U O Y P P P
```

ADAPTATION	ENVIRONMENT	POLYGAMOUS
AFRICA	HABITAT	PREDATOR
CAMOUFLAGE	HUNTER	PREY
CARNIVORE	LIFESPAN	PRIDE
CLAWS	MAMMALS	SAVANNA
CONSERVATION	MANE	SCAVENGE
CUBS	NOCTURNAL	SPECIES

INDEX

adaptations, 11
apex predators, 27
appearance, 7
carnivores, 12
climate change, 27
communication, 23
conservation, 28
cubs, 16, 19
diet, 12
dominant males, 19
eating habits, 12, 15
eyesight, 11, 15
Felidae family, 7
female lions, 15, 16, 19
food chain, 27
fur, 11
gestation, 16
habitat, 8
habitat destruction, 27
humans, 27
hunting, 11, 12, 15
hyenas, 12

lifespan, 24
male lions, 19
mammals, 4
mating, 16
nocturnal, 20
Panthera leo, 4
poaching, 27
population, 24
predators, 27
prey, 12, 15
pride, 19, 23
savanna, 8
scavenge, 12
size, 7
sleep, 20
socialization, 23
speed, 15
sub-Saharan Africa, 4
territory, 19, 23
threats, 27, 28
vocalizations, 23
vulnerable species, 24

Published by Dylanna Press an imprint of Dylanna Publishing, Inc.
Copyright © 2022 by Dylanna Press
Author: Tyler Grady
All rights reserved. No part of this publication may be reproduced, stored in a retrieval system, or transmitted by any means, including electronic, mechanical, photocopying, or otherwise, without prior written permission of the publisher.

Although the publisher has taken all reasonable care in the preparation of this book, we make no warranty about the accuracy or completeness of its content and, to the maximum extent permitted, disclaim all liability arising from its use.

Printed in the U.S.A.

Made in the USA
Las Vegas, NV
05 May 2024

89565861R00019